12 Months of Christmas

A Few Thoughts on . . .
How to Always Remember Him

BARLOW L. PACKER

Copyright 2015 Barlow L. Packer

ISBN 978-1-60645-146-5

Dedicated to . . . our Savior

We all have a hero, example, or friend,
Whose love we think will never end.

Two come to mind at this time of year,
This wonderful season of holiday cheer.

One wears red and rides in a sleigh.
The other wears white and walks both ways.

One fills your stocking with candy so tart,
The other spreads love that fills up your heart.

One wraps his gifts with ribbons and bows,
The other, His gifts, to all He shows.

One has eight reindeer pulling his sleigh,
The other says follow, and I'll lead the way.

One goes to the mall for all men to see;
The Other says simply, have faith in Me.

One wears a hat with a fluffy white ball,
The Other wore thorns, and died for us all.

One, when he comes, not a sound he will make,
The other, He'll cause the whole earth to shake.

One, when it's over, returns to the North Pole;
The Other, won't leave; He lives in man's soul.

This Christmas season will come and go, oh so fast.
Becoming another holiday past;

But His Christmas seasons we will all come to see
Are not just for the year, but for Eternity.

—Curtis Packer, oldest son

INTRODUCTION
CHRISTMAS: A MEANS TO AN END

During the month of December, our personal calendars fill with the tasks and trappings of Christmas celebrations, many of which we design to specifically remember Jesus Christ, whose birth we are celebrating. Throughout the year, we pause each Sunday to worship the Lord, but during the Christmas holidays, the admonition to "always remember Him" flows into every day of the week.

The Christmas season gives us an opportunity to focus more on the life of the Savior and opportunities to serve others. It's a wonderful time of year, but as the Christmas season passes, our thoughts move on to other things.

Before the Christmas fire is cold, it's Super Bowl Sunday, and my thoughts and feelings of Christmas are pushed aside as I pay homage to another "gospel"—and it's not the Gospel of Luke.

On Super Bowl Sunday, instead of remembering how Joseph and Mary went to be taxed, I hear about how to prepare for my own taxes. I hear nothing about the inn being full, unless commentators are complaining about a lack of hotel rooms around the Super Bowl.

I hear nothing about the announcements of heavenly hosts and new stars appearing to proclaim His birth to shepherds in their fields, but only about which NFL "stars" appeared for the pre-game, mid-week media-day.

We are instructed to talk of Christ, rejoice in Christ, preach of Christ, and prophesy of Christ. Why? Because the highest of all ideals are found in the life of the Savior. What we sincerely think and know of the Christ will determine what we are and what we will become. We must make the Son of man our ideal. If we do, when a new Christmas season arrives, it will have been a better year because we will have discovered that no other life will uplift and refine our own as will His.

If we are not careful, it is possible to go the whole month and never find or look for the important parts of Christmas. There are two ways to approach Christmas.

Christmas I is more merry; Christmas II is more manger. Christmas I savors Christmas trappings. Christmas II is about sacred purposes. Christmas I worries about what to give, while Christmas II knows why we give. Christmas I is about extremes. Christmas II wants to return home and enjoy the warmth of a family meal. Christmas I is more "conspicuous consumption," while Christmas II is "charity never faileth," understanding that because of Him redemption is real.

There is a definite contradiction between the two. To nurture Christmas I is to promote and plan first to enjoy yourself. To nurture Christmas II is to confront your weaknesses and help others enjoy themselves.

We live in a world that encourages Christmas I. We're encouraged to think about how to have a great time, but we're unable to cultivate the inner spirit of Christmas. With Christmas I, we become adept at playing the Christmas "game," letting the deepest parts of our Christmas character go unexplored. With Christmas I, we keep ourselves busy while nurturing a vague feeling that, even though it's one of the highlights of our year, the anticipation was greater than the realization. We sometimes wonder, "Is this all there is to it?"

For many years people have talked about how it would be wonderful if the Christmas spirit could extend into other months of the year. Not the shopping and spending of course, but the giving, the service, the gathering, the timeouts and truces of strained relationships. It's about lengthening the tendency that Christmas has to cultivate a generous heart. Keeping that part and, with a breath of kindness, blowing away the rest.

I think I was born with a distinct inclination toward celebrating a Christmas I, then moving on to other things. I'm getting better at doing Christmas II, but during the rest of the year, I struggle, as they say in London, to not only "mind the gap," but close the gap.

This book is about something we experienced as a family over the past few decades, something that evolved serendipitously and has helped us more often to always remember Him.

In its most simple form, all we did was:

1. Choose a place;
2. Take a picture;
3. Search for and find the words of a scripture or a hymn;
4. Using what we discovered, I wrote a related message that helped us (not just in December) to "always remember Him."

Each year this photo and letter became our Christmas card. Each setting, picture, scripture, and message formed a collection of the autobiographical photos and messages in real-life settings, outings, and activities—similar to places you and your family may also have been at sometime.

There is no one better to remember, talk of, think about, and model one's life after than the Savior. Over the centuries, moralists have tried to teach certain standards of living by holding up exemplars. The greatest exemplar of all is Jesus Christ.

For us, each photo and essay is a reminder of the Savior's life and example that helps us keep the feelings of Christ and Christmas in our lives.

It all began in 1977 with a setting, a photo, and a message with a scripture.

1977

A Few Thoughts on... the Rock

As you leave the Salt Lake Valley and drive up Little Cottonwood Canyon, which leads to two of the world's greatest ski resorts, you will see on the right and left sheer walls of granite forming the canyon walls. About a mile into the canyon, you can make a left turn onto a road that leads to an amazing work of engineering—the Granite Mountain Records Vault—simply known as the Vault.

By the side of the road leading up to the vault entrance is a large granite rock, which we refer to simply as "the rock". While sitting on this rock in 1977, we took the first of our Christmas card photos with all five of our children. That rock is still there, solid immovable, and a firm foundation for our photo. In fact, twenty years later, we went back to the same rock for our 1997 photo. We did our best to all sit in the same positions as the first photo, which was a little tricky because the kids had grown.

Like the rock, many things in our lives have remained solid and firm. The Church, His gospel, Him: "the same yesterday, today and forever."

That day in 1977, none of the kids really knew what the next twenty years would bring.

1997

Still rock solid after twenty years were the wishes of two parents who hope the Savior's gospel will always be the rock upon which our kids build their lives—the love we have for each other as a family, our knowledge of His love for us, and the faith we have in eternal family ties.

Because of Him, in a chaotic world, the things that matter most are solid, as he taught, *"Wherefore I am in your midst and I am the good shepherd, and the stone of Israel. He that buildeth upon this rock shall never fail."* (D&C 50:44)

We hope that there are a lot of good, solid, granite-like "rocks" upon which you are building your lives that will come to your mind this Christmas as we always remember Him.

1980

A FEW THOUGHTS ON PLANET EARTH

Most people have a favorite place; somewhere they love to revisit, somewhere that makes their basic metabolic rate slow. When you're there, you feel all is well with the world, and your personality becomes more like you've always wanted it to be.

My place is Grand Teton National Park. As you drive north, about thirteen miles out of Jackson, Wyoming, you can turn west at Moose Junction onto the road that leads to Jenny Lake. About half-way to Jenny Lake, the road makes a sweeping turn to the northeast. If you look northwest, you capture an amazing scenic vista of the Grand Tetons. On this occasion, we pulled over and stopped, the kids got out of the car, and headed for the log tripod fence. Perched on the log rails of the fence, we sat and enjoyed the scene. What a view!

As a young boy, my paper route covered the west side of St. Anthony, Idaho and most mornings, clouds permitting, I had a panoramic view of a Grand Teton sunrise. Later, in college, visiting there with friends, joined by a new bride, we enjoyed rafting, hiking, and climbing, as well as discovering, on horseback, Grand Teton National Park. That area north of Jackson seemed to become part of my DNA.

I wonder if in the next life God could replay how those mountains formed. Be it the Tetons, the Grand Canyon, Lake Powell, Cannon beach, Zion National Park, Yosemite, the Redwoods, or one of a thousand other beautiful places on this earth, I've often stopped to ponder the beauty of His creations.

Many times we take these mortal digs we inhabit for granted but when you look beyond its indescribable beauty, you'll find planet Earth to be an amazing place created to specifically suite our existence.

If there were even slight alterations in the expansion rate of the universe or the strength of its gravitational attraction, life on earth would be impossible. The expansion rate of the universe was an initial condition of creation. It existed from the very beginning, which means that no cosmological evolutionary process can account for it.

In the book *Jesus on Trial* by David Limbaugh, there are several interesting scientific facts that point to an intelligent Creator. A few interesting facts to consider:

1. Protons are positively charged sub-atomic particles that are 1,836 times larger than electrons. If they were slightly larger or smaller, we would not exist, because atoms could not form the molecules required for our existence. If the positive charge of the protons did not balance the electrons, which are a different size, we also would not exist.

2. The unique properties of water are also essential to Earth's habitability. All lifeforms require water, which is unique among substances in that its solid form (ice) is less dense than its liquid form, which causes ice to float. Without this floating property, Earth would freeze beyond the point of human life.

3. The Earth absorbs just the right amount of light and reflects the rest—otherwise we would suffer either from an excess green house effect, or we would freeze.

4. A slight variation in the speed of light would preclude life on Earth.
5. If the Earth's rotation were longer than twenty-four hours, the variation in temperature between day and night would be too great to support life. But if the rotation were shorter, atmospheric wind velocities would be too extreme.

This is only a fraction of the copious scientific evidence today that points to a creator—such an abundance.

As we contemplate the origin of our favorite places, I think of the words, "Behold, here am I," which set in motion the plan to organize all that matter. The "I," of course, being He whose birth we are celebrating.

"Oh Lord, my God, when I in awesome wonder, consider all the worlds thy hands have made. I see the stars, I hear the rolling thunder, Thy power throughout the universe displayed. Then sings my soul, my Savior God to thee. How great thou art, how great thou art." (from Hymn #89, How Great Thou Art)

When Jesus Christ and the Father saw the finished product, and it was all done, God proclaimed:

"And I, God, saw everything that I had made, and behold all things which I had made were very good . . ." (Moses 2:31)

Here's hoping that sometime in the near future, you can return to one of your favorite places on planet Earth.

A Few Thoughts on Reminders of Home

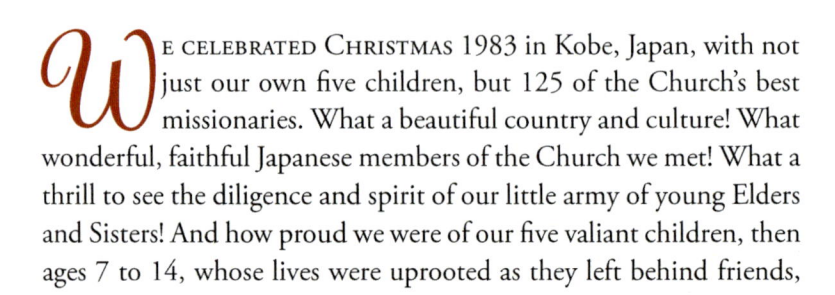

We celebrated Christmas 1983 in Kobe, Japan, with not just our own five children, but 125 of the Church's best missionaries. What a beautiful country and culture! What wonderful, faithful Japanese members of the Church we met! What a thrill to see the diligence and spirit of our little army of young Elders and Sisters! And how proud we were of our five valiant children, then ages 7 to 14, whose lives were uprooted as they left behind friends,

1983

Three of the five kids in the picture, later returned to Japan on their own full-time missions.

cousins, schools, and who, for the next three years, missed out on the traditional youth experiences they would have had back home.

In place of those missed opportunities, they had the opportunity to experience many great new ones. They attended an international school, the Canadian Academy, where the primary language spoken in class was English. This allowed them to make friends with kids from all over the world whose parents were in Kobe because of their various international vocations.

When we celebrated the birthday of one of our sons, a small group of his friends were invited to the Mission Home for a party. As they began calling their parents to come pick them up afterward, one spoke to his parents in French, another in German, another in Norwegian, and another in Afrikaans.

One blessing we appreciated during our experience in Japan was that, outside of school hours, most of our children's evenings and weekends were spent with each other. They became each other's best friends despite the age differences. Twenty-five years later, that is still evident as adult siblings when we're all together as a family.

One Saturday, shortly after arriving in Japan, we took the kids on an outing downtown to the center of Kobe. As we found a place to park and were walking around taking in the sights and atmosphere of a very busy Japanese Saturday afternoon, we came around a corner that opened onto a large intersection where several thoroughfares merged. Lo and behold, across the way rose up two familiar Golden Arches.

"Hey, Mom and Dad! Look! A McDonald's!"

They could hardly wait for the lights to change so we could navigate the giant intersection. Needless to say a "great" meal was enjoyed by all. During the meal you would have thought we were sitting in the McDonald's back home at Highland Drive and Ft. Union Blvd—Salt Lake or Japan, they're all pretty much the same.

Regardless of what many may think of the quality of food at McDonald's, to our little tribe that day, in a new country, feeling akin to the Israelites wandering for what seemed like forty years in the desert, their meal was like manna (a Big Mac) from heaven and water (Sprite) bursting forth from a rock!

That afternoon was a wonderful reminder to our kids of things home, of things stable, of things they would certainly return to. But we also hope they learned that this season in their young lives is a great blessing that will prepare them for things to come.

"Teach ye diligently and my grace shall attend you, that you may be instructed more perfectly in theory, in principle, in doctrine . . . Of things both in heaven and in the earth, and under the earth; things which have been, things which are, things which must shortly come to pass; things which are at home, things which are abroad; the wars and the perplexities of the nations, and the judgments which are on the land; and a knowledge also of countries and of kingdoms—

That ye may be prepared in all things when I shall send you again to magnify the calling whereunto I have called you, and the mission with which I have commissioned you. (D&C 88: 78-80)

1984

Behind the camera when this picture was taken, were about one hundred Japanese people who had gathered to watch and wonder what this American family was doing (with permission from the conductor of the bullet train), taping Christmas stockings to the nose of the Bullet train.

A Few Thoughts on the Speed of Life

A FORMER OLYMPIAN LONG distance runner made a living helping others prepare for "running" events such as 5K's, 10K's and marathons. He specialized in older clients who were past their athletic prime—people like me who have, as they say, "lost a step," or a lot of steps, which is why his approach was very unique.

He showed, and his data backed it up, that sometimes slower is better. Meaning that short walking intervals during your race allow your body to "recover" physiologically and can actually lead to a faster overall time than if you ran the full distance.

Why? Because the short periods of recovery allow you to run faster while you are running. Even though you slow to a walk for intervals throughout your race, the sum total is faster than if you tried to keep running the whole distance.

It's like sitting in your car, progressing slowly through a myriad of orange cones forming your path, when you see a very insightful sign that says, "By going slow now, you can go faster later."

I liken this same principle to how we celebrate the Christmas holidays. Every year, as the Christmas season approaches, the speed of life increases. It's like a month of flipping to the "accelerate" position on our car's "cruise" control lever. We speed up, hit set, cruise for a while, and then for some reason, we have to hit the brakes and slow down. Then we flick the lever to the "resume speed" position again, and off we go.

We're busy shopping and planning our holidays when, on our calendar, there appears a lovely evening for a Christmas dinner with longtime friends. We hit the brakes, slow down, enjoy the evening, and then, the next morning we flip the "resume speed" lever and off we go again until the next slow down. Before we know it, we're saying "where did that last month go? I can't believe it's over," as the cascade of seasonal retail hype we are subjected to diminishes back to normal levels.

Without those occasional "slow" intervals among the "rush," we wouldn't have enjoyed the holidays nearly as much.

In Japan we rode the Bullet Train several times. I can just say one thing. Wow! On a schedule you can set your watch by, the Bullet Train pulls in, stops, and the doors open.

Once on the train, what a ride! The Bullet Trains in Japan run entirely on elevated tracks, avoiding the risk of ground level railroad crossings. Computerized safety systems have resulted in zero accidents or passenger injuries to date. About 46 percent of the line has been tunneled through difficult terrain rather than around, for the most direct routes at high speed. The bullet trains travel at around 130 plus miles per hour between stops.

There are two types of trains: the "Kodama," (Japanese for "turtle") which stops at every station, and the "Hikari" (Japanese for "flash"), which stops only at certain stations, roaring through the station at full speed. What an experience to be standing on the platform of a Bullet Train station when a Hikari comes roaring through without stopping.

We live in societies that place great importance on getting somewhere fast, either by train or on wider multi-lane freeways. It's nice, even during the Christmas season's Hikari-like pace, to be more "Kodama-like," stopping at more "stations" to enjoy the day.

One day when I was zipping along the countryside in Japan on the Bullet Train to Kyoto to speak to missionaries gathering for a Zone Conference, I couldn't help but think that He whose message I had prepared to teach, *walked* most everywhere He went.

What really matters, as we think about the speed of life during the Christmas season, isn't how fast we get from point A to point B. What matters is that we enjoy the ride, knowing that His birth, His life, and His message will help us know that our "Point B" during the holidays (or any other time of the year) is the right destination.

It may help to slow the speed of life by stopping to *"remember the Lord their God, and to give ear unto his counsels, to walk in wisdom's paths!"* (Helaman 12:5)

We would all do well to take advantage of those "rest stops" we fly by on the Interstate, and as the Savior said, *"Come follow (or remember) me all ye that are heavy laden (rushed) and I will give you rest."* (Matthew 11:28)

A Few Thoughts on "Life Elevated"

With duct tape and Christmas stockings in hand, we were off to Snowbird in December 1986. Having lived in the Salt Lake Valley most of my life and having skied at the resorts in the Big and Little Cottonwood Canyons since I was in the seventh grade, I had gained an appreciation for those mountains and the panoramic beauty you can see when you get off a ski lift or the tram at Snowbird and do a 360 degree look-about.

Every one of us in this modern work-a-day world needs, maybe just a moment, a few hours, or sometimes a couple of days of rest and recovery without having to get on a plane or drive all day to get there.

1986

We need to stop and appreciate whatever unique beauty surrounds us, because it can be easy to forget in the bustle of our busy lives.

We saw it all from the top of the tram. Standing and enjoying the scene as family, it was great to see such a view. On Mount Analog, Rene Dumal made an interesting observation, "You cannot stay on the summit forever, you have to come down again. So, why bother in the first place? Just this: What is above knows what is below, but what is below does not know what is above. One climbs, one sees, one descends; one sees no longer, but one has seen."

Marilyn Fergeson responded to Dumal's thought, "there is a real art to governing one's life in the lower regions, by the memory of what one saw higher up." There are lots of "higher ups" in our lives in the form of great mountains and beautiful vistas, but also in the form of family, good friends, and the love of He whose birth we are celebrating. Especially at Christmas, it's important to remember there is an art of governing oneself in the lower regions by the memory of what one saw higher up.

So having descended from our Christmas highs, I wish the things we saw and felt during the Christmas season would linger a little longer.

And the Lord did show me from time to time after what manner I should work the timbers of the ship.

Now I, Nephi, did not work the timbers after the manner which was learned by men, neither did I build the ship after the manner of men; but I did build it after the manner which the Lord had shown unto me; wherefore, it was not after the manner of men.

And I, Nephi, did go into the mount oft, and I did pray oft unto the Lord; wherefore the Lord showed unto me great things. (1 Nephi 17: 1-3)

Isn't it reassuring to know, because of the One who descended below all things, we can learn to govern ourselves below? We know that because of Him, we can again ascend higher than we ever imagined to see and learn, as did Nephi, indescribable things. I'm glad Christmas is a "higher up" holiday.

A Few Thoughts on "Breaking Bread"

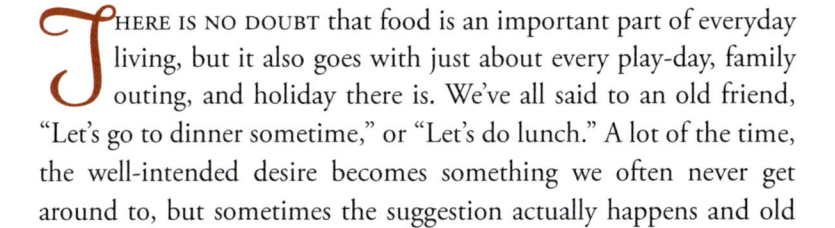

THERE IS NO DOUBT that food is an important part of everyday living, but it also goes with just about every play-day, family outing, and holiday there is. We've all said to an old friend, "Let's go to dinner sometime," or "Let's do lunch." A lot of the time, the well-intended desire becomes something we often never get around to, but sometimes the suggestion actually happens and old relationships are revitalized.

There are lists that have been published of the best kinds of restaurants to take a client to for that "power lunch" and more recently the "power breakfast."

Of course we have heard about the ever famous "free lunch," which tradition says is a myth, as "there is no such thing as a free lunch."

Then there is the "coffee" break, which has grown beyond coffee to protein drinks, 5-hour energy shots, and Diet Coke.

1990

What would a ballgame be without a hot-dog, or tortilla chips smothered in cheese; a movie without popcorn; or a picnic in the canyon without fried chicken?

There is hardly a gathering with friends, family, or co-workers where great food isn't part of the mix, as we test, taste, and try out everyone's homemade Christmas goodies. In fact, by the end the holidays, our dining room table is loaded with paper plates covered with Saran wrap, representing a cascade of homemade calories left on our doorstep by wonderful neighbors.

What is also cool is that, as we receive, partake, enjoy, and even gain weight, part of our indulgence is the active remembering of others who are not so blessed. And as we remember He whose birth we are celebrating, we too can act as He did in helping others less fortunate experience their own parable of the loaves and fishes.

Because as we look at the "menus" life offers us, we remember that the measure we give is the measure we receive, as we feel the joy that comes from understanding that with all of the abundant breads we enjoy during the holidays, *that man does not live by bread alone,* but bread broken and shared with others. In our own small way, we are emulating the Savior as we feed others, especially those in need.

And Jesus took the loaves; and when he had given thanks, he distributed to the disciples, and the disciples to them that were set down; and likewise of the fishes as much as they would.

When they were filled, he said unto his disciples, Gather up the fragments that remain, that nothing be lost.

Therefore they gathered them together, and filled twelve baskets with the fragments of the five barley loaves, which remained over and above unto them that had eaten. (John 6: 11-13)

The Lord demonstrated that, as we give of our plenty to others, we will always have leftovers—though not always in the form of food. Beware however, that depending on what "bread" we are breaking, we are often full long before our brain signals us that we should stop eating. Don't forget to share.

A Few Thoughts on Simple Pleasures

Some of life's greatest gifts are simple pleasures overlooked. Often in pursuit of "stuff," we fail to partake in some of the simple joys. One advocate of simplicity called the ability to enjoy simple things "the only way to be rich."

The enjoyment of simple ordinary pleasures requires a keen sense of living in the moment. One of the profound rewards of this enhanced attention to the simple—and even small—pleasures is the discovery of how much we really have.

The spirit of the Christmas season, if we focus on what really matters, helps deepen our appreciation for the valuables we often misplace.

There are good books, beautiful music, neglected hobbies or talents, gentle, relaxing exercise, inspiring scenery, small acts of service, and the comfort of an old rocker. I've found that being alone with my own thoughts, thinking things through, pondering and seeking answers, made my drive back and forth to work as valuable as any other time of the day. But I had to turn off the car radio to discover such a simple pleasure.

"*Let no man count them as small things; for there is much which lieth in futurity, pertaining to the saints, which depends upon these things.* (D&C 123:15)

Now ye may suppose that this is foolishness in me; but behold I say unto you, that by small and simple things are great things brought to pass; . . . (Alma 37:6)

I hope you find something simple to re-enjoy; a favorite book to re-read, a classic movie to re-watch, or even an old dusty guitar to re-stimulate the little calluses on your fingertips.

1995

1998

A Few Thoughts on Conversation

Nineteen-ninety-eight was a big year for us. After three weddings in five months, we took a family recovery junket to Bear Lake during the summer. Unlike previous getaways there, this time we had two new daughters-in-law and a new son-in-law.

As we relaxed around the cabin and on the beach, we mostly just talked. It became a fun adventure in conversation. We tried to out-tell each others' stories and even "outed" our kids, giving their new spouses lots of details from their childhood that they would've rather we not shared. It became a "conversation space," a term I learned about in the book, *Life Coaching: A Manual for Helping Professionals* by Dave Ellis.

He explained that we can reshape relationships, our work, and other segments of our lives if we properly manage our "conversation spaces." Ellis defined "conversation" with others or ourselves, as any occurrence of thinking, pondering, writing, listening, watching, or talking—noting that talking with others face to face is only one type of conversation. Watching television is another, even if only one-sided (unless you're yelling at the TV set because you're watching a sports game or political pundits).

Other types of "conversation" may include reading a newspaper, writing a letter, preparing a talk, listening to the radio, reading a good book, being in a meeting, daydreaming, or watching a sunset. All of these "conversational spaces" involve exposure to information, ideas, and reactions we feel and think about.

But most importantly, these activities take up a lot of "space" in our lives and make up a lot of what we do each day. Moment by moment, we make choices about where to place our attention, outwardly or inwardly. Every second presents us with an opportunity to choose our conversations—what we listen to; talk about; who we talk with; and what we watch, read, or think about.

As we spent time together, all adults, as a newly expanded family, and talked and talked, we listened and grew to love each other more. It was perfect management of our "conversational space." And what made it even more perfect was that, from time to time, the conversation touched on the importance in their lives of He whose birth we are celebrating; He who taught us something we should strive for as a family.

"Art thou a brother or brethren? I salute you in the name of the Lord Jesus Christ, in token or remembrance of the everlasting

Same place twenty-one years earlier before daughters- and sons-in-law...

covenant, in which covenant I receive you to fellowship, in a determination that is fixed, immovable, and unchangeable, to be your friend and brother through the grace of God in the bonds of love, to walk in all the commandments of God blameless, in thanksgiving, forever and ever. Amen." (D&C 88:133)

We hope you will find wonderful opportunities for uplifting "conversational spaces" and that you remember that the celebration of His birth is what brings us together with loved ones.

2001

A FEW THOUGHTS ON THE ROAD TO CHARACTER

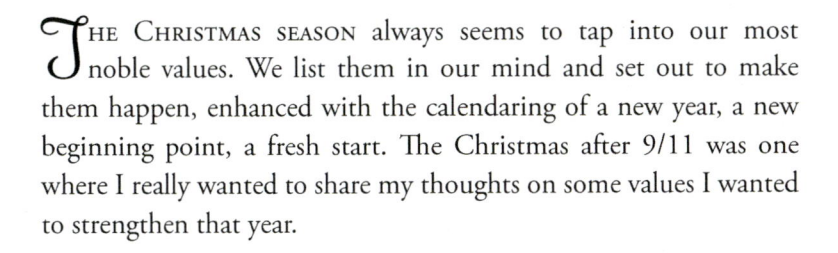

THE CHRISTMAS SEASON always seems to tap into our most noble values. We list them in our mind and set out to make them happen, enhanced with the calendaring of a new year, a new beginning point, a fresh start. The Christmas after 9/11 was one where I really wanted to share my thoughts on some values I wanted to strengthen that year.

1. Never confuse life with work, because the second is only a portion of the first.
2. Never let work get in the way of being a good parent or grandparent.
3. Pay more attention to—and enjoy—the little things, such as the expression of concentration on the face of a new grandson as he tries to pick up a single Cheerio with his thumb and index finger off his highchair tray.
4. Never let a group of five or eleven athletes determine your mood or how happy you are.
5. Remember that it's okay to eat as much as you want if you're eating the right things.
6. Make a few more "just called to see how you're doing" phone calls; actually "do lunch" a few times with friends; and take the time to write a few more letters and thank you notes.
7. Remember that sleep is always more restful if you've exercised that day.
8. Be more grateful for friends and spouses. Without them, no one would be interested in what you have to say.
9. Make others feel funnier, smarter, and better about themselves when they are with you.

The road to character isn't the road to perfection. Character is being someone who will answer softly when challenged harshly; one who can even remain silent when unfairly blamed; one who remains dignified when others are trying to humiliate them. Essentially, character is just trying to be more like He whose birth we are celebrating.

"And when he was accused of the chief priests and elders, he answered nothing.

Then said Pilate unto him, Hearest thou not how many things they witness against thee? And he answered him to never a word; insomuch that the governor marveled greatly." (Matthew 27:11-14)

Character is a long road, but Christmas give us a reason to make the journey. So no matter what difficulties and challenges life presents, drop your attitude into 4-wheel drive, and "keep on truckin."

2003

A Few Thoughts on Pencils

Have you noticed the explosion of high-tech toys? Laptops are almost mundane today with the newer hand-held smart phones recently joining the scene. Also, with digital cameras, we can shoot the picture, download, upload, and email it; then crop it, tweak the colors, add or remove someone from the picture, and even print it at home, in color.

We can watch hundreds of cable channels, stream hundreds of movies and old sitcoms at home on our new smart TV, or on the go, from our iPad or smart phone.

It's amazing what has developed as a result of GPS. We can track our distance, pace, heart rate, and number of steps we take. And with our phone, or in our car, we are guided turn by turn, over the river and through the woods to grandmother's house. Cars can now call 911 for you if you're in an accident, help you locate the car if it's stolen, and unlock itself for you if you lose your keys.

And FWIW (for what it's worth), terms like CD, HDTV, DSL, GPS, FAX, LCD, DVD, have turned our language into a sort of alphabet soup. What ever happened to DOS?

One day I needed to make list of things to do. Rummaging around in one of my desk drawers, I found an unsharpened #2 Ticonderoga yellow pencil that gave me a surge of de'ja vu. I recalled a fable about an old pencil maker. He took a pencil aside just before putting it into its box for shipping.

"There are five things you need to know to be a good pencil. One, you will be able to accomplish many great things if you allow yourself to be held in a writer's hand. Two, you will experience a painful sharpening from time to time, but it will make you a better pencil. Three, you will be able to correct any mistakes you might make. Four, remember the most important part of you is what is inside. And five, no matter what, on every surface you are used on, try to leave your best mark and continue to write."

It's reassuring to know, as we remember He whose birth we are celebrating, it's worth striving to let Him hold us in His hand, let Him help us get through those difficult sharpenings. Remember that He has shown us how to correct our mistakes and know that He loves us because of what we are inside, not for what we have, or own. Remember, especially during Christmas, that we can reach out to others and leave our mark, and with His help, keep on "writing."

"This they said, tempting him, that they might have to accuse him. But Jesus stooped down, and with his finger wrote on the ground, as though he heard them not.

So when they continued asking him, he lifted up himself, and said unto them, He that is without sin among you, let him first cast a stone at her. And again he stooped down, and wrote on the ground." (John 6:6-8)

High tech toys are fun, but once in awhile, it's nice to remember there are simple tools you can drum on a desk top, twiddle in your fingers, or chew on if you are nervous. There are gifts that won't be broken if dropped, that aren't expensive to replace if broken and, like most pencils, don't need to be recharged.

The Packer Dental Group
Barlow L. Packer D.D.S.
Gardiner M. Packer D.D.S.
McKay B. Packer D.D

2004

A Few Thoughts on Work

We all spend a significant amount of our lives at work in order to buy the things we want or need.

Like anything else in life, there is plenty of free advice (minus the price of the book or DVD) from people standing next to their pool, mansion, Lear jet or Rolls Royce. They promise the "lifestyle you deserve," in only two or three hours a week from your kitchen table, for only four payments of $29.95, automatically withdrawn from your credit card. And within a few short weeks, you'll be able to quit your real job and lounge around your pool, opening envelopes with checks that arrive daily in the mail.

Then there are those who wax philosophical, making you feel like something is wrong with you if your "work isn't your play," and if you just "do what you love, the money will follow."

No matter what our work is, don't we all look forward to the weekend? Don't we all treasure the rewards of spending time with family, friends, hobbies, play, and even puttering around our home, yards, and gardens?

That's why we enjoy Christmas so much. As we put work on the back burner, we focus more on the non-material elements of life. We enjoy having children back home, time with old friends, and Christmas worship, Christmas music, the Christmas ambience of our homes, and the charitable acts of helping those less fortunate.

We experience this truth: the anticipation of material things is always greater than their realization, but the anticipation of spiritual things is always exceeded by their realization.

Sooner than we would like, the weekend, the vacation, and the holidays are over. But even on the first Monday in January, the words of He whose birth we celebrated can change our perspective and help us sense more of the non-material or spiritual elements of our work.

Even at work, we can find ways to learn and grow. *("And he that received two talents…gained two other talents.")* We can better love those we work with. *("In as much as ye have done it unto one of the least…ye have done it unto me.")* We can better serve those who would buy our product or service, as *"cast thy bread upon the waters."*

And we can enjoy the satisfaction of giving our best as we find that *"The sleep of the laboring man is sweet."*

"And behold, I, the Lord, declare unto you, and my words are sure and shall not fail, that they shall obtain it. But all things must come to pass in their time. Wherefore, be not weary in well-doing, for ye are laying the foundation of a great work. And out of small things proceedeth that which is great. Behold, the Lord requireth the heart and a willing mind; and the willing and obedient shall eat the good of the land of Zion in these last days. (D&C 64:31-34)

So when the time comes that it's again, "Hi ho, hi ho, it's off to work we go," let's "whistle while we work," as we anticipate the next weekend, or holiday, knowing that its reality will exceed its anticipation.

2007

A Few Thoughts on Spoiling Grandkids

In the pursuit of true happiness and wealth, a wise man once said: "Ancient rites placed one goal and one delight above all others, the joy in one's posterity." He was telling us that the ultimate delight is to be in the company of one's own flesh and blood, which is the wonder, glory, and burden, of our existence.

Ultimately it is our posterity who give us the greatest sense of true wealth and happiness. Investing our time and money spoiling our grandkids, as one advocate called it, is "the only way to be rich."

Our photos taken with grandchildren portray the current asset column of our family financial statement. It's hard to calculate the true net worth of this little gathering of bare feet, but since becoming grandparents, we've come to appreciate the new form of financial planning. It's called creative capitalism, or in other words: Grandma and Grandpa is the name, and "spoiling's" our game!

To promote this form of financial planning, may we offer a few suggestions about this joyful form of economics:

1. When your grandchildren are in your care, never truly obey bedtime and nap instructions given by their parents. After all, what do they know?

    Note: At our house we fake it. They are usually in bed on time, even early, but it's our king size bed, alll together with pillows and popcorn, watching anyone of a hundred DVDs they have seen many times before, but still like to watch. They are usually asleep before the movie is finished.

2. Always remember that grandma's cherished Beanie Baby collection is to play with, not to be placed on the shelf to look at. Naps and bedtime are always better with Beanie Babies.

3. It is always okay to turn on and play with the water hose in the yard.

    Note: Remember, water dries, and there are some great water toys you can buy to attach to the hose. Warning: you may have to get a little wet yourself.

4. Always have fun with music. Children love to dance and twirl with grandma and grandpa.

5. Have at least three different cookie jars, plenty of juice, and at least four options of cold cereal as the bare minimum to properly nourish visiting grandchildren.

    Note: Don't ever run out of milk.

6. A library of at least fifty children's books are required.

    Note: They always snuggle closer or sit on your lap when you offer to read a story or look at pictures in a book.

7. Don't throw away the old Fisher Price toys you bought for your own kids. They're still in. They really get you "down to their level" on the carpet.

8. Make sure you have brightly-colored alphabet refrigerator magnets on the refrigerator door so they can spell their name—or just play there on the floor of the kitchen, putting them on and off, again, and again, and again.

9. Keep on hand a large basket of various balls: tennis, rubber, or Nerf (one's that don't hurt when they hit you).

10. Plan on the fact that kids may not eat everything on their plate. Be prepared for intermittent "re-fueling" stops rather than a one-sitting fueling stop to fill up.

    Note: Paper plates and cups are great.

11. If your knees and back are healthy, horseback rides that lead to being bucked off onto the sofa are a hit. You should have plenty of blankets available for building caves, hideouts, and huts between and behind the sofas and chairs.

Note: A few in-expensive flashlights from Home Depot and any old cell phones add to the ambience.

12. Be sure to have a swing if possible in your yard. Peacefully being swung lulls a lot of grandchildren into a very mellow mood.

Whether you use your own list or some of our ideas, remember that these gifts of time are a simple way to spoil grandkids. It's a modern-day version of the gold, frankincense, and myrrh that were given in love to the Child whose birth we are celebrating.

As Paul wrote to Timothy: *"…my dearly beloved son: Grace, mercy, and peace, from God the Father and Christ Jesus our Lord. When I call to remembrance the unfeigned faith that is in thee, which dwelt first in thy grandmother Lois, and thy mother Eunice; and I am persuaded that in thee also. Wherefore I put thee in remembrance that thou stir up the gift of God, (in our grandchildren) which is in thee by the putting on of my hands. For God hath not given us (grandparents) the spirit of fear; but of power, and of love, and of a sound mind."* (2 Timothy 1:4-7)

As grandparents we must never underestimate the influence for good we can be to the children of our children.

Conclusion

Looking for Life's Capo D'Astro Bar

THERE'S A STORY about a man named Bud Robbins. He worked at an ad agency, and he was asked by the president of the company to create an ad campaign. Their client was the Aeolian Piano Company, and the first ad was to run in the *New York Times*.

After a two-day tour of the factory to learn more about the Aeolian piano, Robbins had discovered nothing unique. Robbins said as much to the company's national sales manager, who then took him into a beautiful showroom. There, elegantly arranged, were three pianos. An Aeolian, between a comparably priced Baldwin and Steinway.

"They sure do look alike," Robbins commented.

"They sure do. About the only difference is the shipping weight," replied the sales manager.

"Heavier?" asked Mr. Robbins, "What makes the Aeolian heavier?"

"The capo d' astro bar."

When Robbins asked what a capo d'astro bar was, the sales manager told him to look under the piano. He pointed to a metallic bar fixed across the harp and bearing down on the highest octaves. He explained that it takes fifty years before the harp in the piano starts to warp.

"That's when the capo d' astro bar goes to work," said the sales manager.

"You mean the capo d' astro bar doesn't go to work for fifty years?"

"Well, there has to be some reason why the Metropolitan Opera uses our piano."

Robbins dove under the Baldwin to find a tinkertoy capo d' astro bar at best; and the same under the Steinway.

"In fact," continued the sales manager, "Rise Stevens, who is in charge of moving the Met to the new Lincoln Center, says about the only thing the Met is taking with them is their piano."

That quote was the headline for the *New York Times* ad which resulted in a six-year wait between order and delivery.

In many organizations, products, and especially in people's lives, you sense the presence of a kind of "capo d' astro bar" within their character. It's something that sets that person apart from the world. It's that something that keeps us from "warping." What we sincerely think and know of the Christ will determine who we are and what we will become. We must make the Son of man our ideal. We must do all we can to not only emulate the one perfect being who ever walked the earth, but always try to recognize and see His hand in our lives, even when it's not Christmas. With mercy, love, and compassion, He took upon Himself the sins of the world and satisfied the necessity of justice for all who will always remember Him. As Elder Quentin L. Cook said in a General Conference address, "Like the young sunflower, when we follow the Savior of the world, the Son of God, we flourish and become glorious, despite the many terrible circumstances that surround us. He is truly our light and life."

We don't have to enjoy the feelings of Christmas just in December if we look for evidence, connections to, likenings of, or examples of His life in the daily, often mundane, living of our own life.

I have learned through all of our Christmas card messages and photo experiences, that our ability to stand firm and true in following the Savior, in spite of the worldly crucible of life, is greatly strengthened by looking for and discovering evidence of Him in all we do.

Christ is the capo d' astro bar of our lives, and as we all feel the pressure of worldly warping beginning to increase, because of Him we needn't bend an inch if we can find a way, all year long, to always remember Him.

Made in the USA
Middletown, DE
26 December 2016